3...2..1. FOCUS

A manual for concentration amid chaos

Bhaskar Sengupta

Ukiyoto Publishing

All global publishing rights are held by

Ukiyoto Publishing

Published in 2024

Content Copyright © Bhaskar Sengupta
ISBN 9789362691590

*All rights reserved.
No part of this publication may be reproduced, transmitted, or stored in a retrieval system, in any form by any means, electronic, mechanical, photocopying, recording or otherwise, without the prior permission of the publisher.*

The moral rights of the author have been asserted.

This is a work of fiction. Names, characters, businesses, places, events, locales, and incidents are either the products of the author's imagination or used in a fictitious manner. Any resemblance to actual persons, living or dead, or actual events is purely coincidental.

This book is sold subject to the condition that it shall not by way of trade or otherwise, be lent, resold, hired out or otherwise circulated, without the publisher's prior consent, in any form of binding or cover other than that in which it is published.

www.ukiyoto.com

"The difference between an ordinary person and an extra-ordinary person is the degree of concentration"

_____*Swami Vivekananda*

Dedicated to my parents whatever I am is because of their blessings

Introduction

This book Is for those who wants to be at theIr absolute best at all life- sItuatIons. ThIs book will gIve a holIstIc perspectIve of How, Why & When to focus.

A consolidation of almost all the major focus techniques & their user manual.

Over-coming past/ chIldhood trauma with realistic solutions. This book is a journey from childhood trauma- deciphering It & then overcoming It-Applying scientific techniques to become best versions of ourselves.

It is an user-manual of focus/memory/productivity hacks.

It's written in an unconventional manner to be precise, applicable & less time-consumIng for the readers.

So, happy reading. This humongous labour will be justified, If readers achieve their desired focus/ success in this devastatingly distracting era of our existence.

Contents

Reading + Writing-	1
Child hood trauma, OCD, Family, Relationships, Friends-	4
Patterns of Disruptions/Repeated Chaotic Events-	10
Saying 'No'/ Making People Unhappy-	12
Struggle(in + out)/ Regimental approach-	14
Meditation-	17
Mind-mapping-	19
Mnemonics-	23
Sub-Concious Mind-	26
Work-Out-	30
DOSE-[THE REWARD CIRCUIT]-	32
Habit Formation/ Getting shit done-	39
Pleasing only thyself / Stop being a people pleaser-	41
Diversify-	43
Understanding Brains Formation-	45
Memory-	45
Emergency studying-	53
Fear of failure/ Unwanted eventualities-	55
Honest to thyself-	56
Focus Techniques-	58
Psychadelics/Nootropics/Mind Renewal-	59
Nootropics-	61

Patanjali's yogasutra-	67
Nutrition for Memory	71
Anki-method-	75
10000 Hour Rule-	78
Peroration	81
About the Author	*82*

Reading + Writing-

- First things first there is no substitute of hard work and studying.
- Read as much as you can on daily basis [even if you read only one page => read.
- Monitor your progress by time stated targets [small target but monitor it.]
- Whatever you read if you want to memorise it completely or selectively=.>Write-down the same without looking at it on a white paper after reading the concerned topic (2-4 times based on your perception capability).
- After writing it read the same topic again and again & rectify the faltered portion if any by your own hands=>This would be done when you need to recall a document/data etc. verbatim.
- This yields long term memory formation in shorter periods of time.
- Over the period you will develop greater efficiency in the said methodology & your time and perception of the brain will improve & in few months you will be amazed by your enhanced capabilities.

Speed reading + Speed writing

- Practice + Practice+Practice-

- Over a considerable period of time (based on where you stand while implementing the methods discussed here) => You will develop rather you develop new neural connections for speed reading capabilities. => If you intentionally try to read faster along with perceiving the topic concerned=> you will master the art of reading fast=> your brain will be able to learn to read the important portions & churn out the un important portions.

- I know the above mentioned portions seems boring/ mundane but this process is somewhat self-propelled mechanism, you will have to get your hands dirty to get the reward.

- If followed will give an edge over competitor's & save the most precious thing in the world =>Time.

- This world is a war among humans=> specially who are in creative, competitive sports, academics, busyness etc. to out done each other in doing boring work/self-work on daily basis, the more you can enjoy the so called boring work the more magical your long term progress becomes.

- It's actually unreal the way achievers at times perform in their respective field that denizen think they are Superhuman.

- However, there are a few gifted invidual who can do a lot so called tough tasks at ease but they are very few & the concern of the individual should be to achieve best version of himself/herself & while doing so a considerable number of people becomes special.
- Furthermore, if anyone can achieve best versions of themselves it's in itself a success.
- Speed writing is also important to save time and train the brain to learn/ perceive/express in shorter span of time.
- It is severely beneficial for memory formation + retention + most importantly utilization.
- A good memory can be described as => faster perception alongwith longterm retention & faster utilization/ recalling.
- In order to do so speed reading(retention)+ speed writing is the by product of harbouring a healthy memory.

Child hood trauma, OCD, Family, Relationships, Friends-

This aspect of the human psychology/neurology is by far the most important & completely neglected portion.

• In order to completely explain/ understand the nuances of this topic- it needs one (affected person) to understand one (another affected person).

• A therapist might explain or try to mitigate the same but it's an inner journey=> only the person concerned can release himself/herself from it.

• Childhood is the time when psychologically and neurologically we are at the most naïve and vulnerable stage.

• Any encouragement in this times amplifies the emotional response from the brain which in turn activates the reward circuit in the brain & the said child is more likely & fiercely will try to do the said task again & again.

• The equally if not more devastating negative response is initiated and embedded in child's brain=> if reprimanded for any task=> or more importantly while doing that task or after the task is done any unforeseen, unfortunate(e.g.- death of loved ones, natural calamity, any ruthless inhuman behaviour, some loss of material/ social nature, some external bad influence, loosing something valuable etc.), traumatising thing happens in that child's life or his family members/loved one's that child will be traumatised for life => whenever some task/similar pattern of events occur if not treated/ emotions released.

• Not only trauma from others many a time an abusive parent, loved one's creates trauma in a naive mind=> let's state it humans never understands others pain in complete rigour & authentic form if they do not face the same=> being selfish/jealous/ sibling rivalry etc.=> creates events which pulverise the naive child/childlike minds for life.

• OCD (OBSESSIVE COMPULSIVE DISOREDER)- This is a socially unexpected/unwanted repeated behaviour/ritual that a humongous proportions of humans secretly share. => which is nothing but brains faulty coping up mechanism which in the hazy perception of the affected individuals mind mitigates or neutralizes the negative/ harmful thoughts for very short period of time & it becomes drastically short spans ranging to even micro seconds in the brain.

• It's like if I do something whether the habit/ritual/behaviour it can be anything (might be something concerning, 'n'=1,2,3...infinity. number of times or clearing hands, saying some words etc.].

- Mind creates perpetual trauma/fear & over the period of time it engulfs the life of a healthy human being.

- Some individual's presence makes or associated with misdeeds/events & you become scared each time. People come and go but they mark their good or bad impression in a child's even adult brains.

- Especially if you're a person who wants everyone's good, who are empathetic towards others=> most of the chances are you are you are the most vulnerable/ affected person=> prey of selfish actions of others.

- In my understanding the people who are more empathetic towards others are most prone to be mentally destabilized, traumatised & depressive in this brutal competitive jungle called human civilization.

- Ruthless selfish, back-stabbing bastards are severe socio-paths or hidden psychopath who don't become mad in front of society because they thrive on people's sufferings & prey on the weak minds=> strategically destroying it is their elixir to repeat the process.

- Solution-

- Nothing can be taught or erased in this spectrum of psychological construct.

- But a warrior's heart knows how to fight & kill

these garbage emotions.

• Therapist may help or facilitate the recovery by therapy, hypnosis, medications, anti-depressants like, Benzodiazepine, but it's you who will make the journey.

My solutions (yes you can win)

Learn any martial art which-

• Requires you to be in combative practices/sports/practice=> the discipline is a trauma/fear killer=> You will feel empowered, reassured=>every problems

• solution will be Brocken down and strategically solved in your mind.

Workout regularly-

• Eat good food (whatever your body craves/wants/needs your brain will let you know & let me give you a well-kept secret of strong men , they eat a lot and they

• eat what their mind wants it's just they burn it & maintain a rigorous workout routine along with cardio=> your body needs almost everything in right proportions so let your brain be the judge of it not any dietician article=>provided that you don't eat any allergic/substance addiction/ or any diabetic food(if your diabetic) or any co-morbidity affecting food & you maintain your regular workout.

Meditate-

- Many sources are available online+ offline follow one which suits you=> it will increase happy hormones.

- Most effective-

- Face the bull by its horns=> do whatever it takes to release those tensions/emotions=> be in that moment=> be in front of that bastard/person & confront boldly=> end it or destroy it from your mind if it requires actions of epic proportions, do it with herculean rigour=> if anyone did wrong you should confront/ combat it in appropriate manner.

- The saying that forgive but do not forget=> if you can't forget, that means you haven't forgiven or released the emotions=> releasing it is the shortest way to reclaim your life. => remember whatever we think or do has its consequences so calibrate/calculate the same & take reasonable actions.

- If you can't reproduce the above mentioned situation, action/event/person then just share the event in any reliable public/ social forum expose the person or event & afterwards show pity/ ignorance to the same and enlighten others like you so that no one falls prey and act accordingly to these sort of situations, it will mature and you will be- bigger/stronger & conqueror of your trauma.

- Life is a war and the war will continue, it's your duty to fight, fight & fight with positive and just intentions.

- Another way is to build your career in such a height that trauma/person/event will be severely irrelevant or weak in front of your conviction/character.

Patterns of Disruptions/Repeated Chaotic Events-

- This is a pattern in our chaotic existence, whether we admit or not, understand or not.

- You are scared traumatized cause you know what series of events occur come fourth if you do certain things, do something to progress/Prosper-It's a catch 22 situation.

- Chao's cannot be stopped but it can be used or tamed to your favour.

- Be that good, regimental in your regular deeds that nothing can shake or break you=>'understand the nature of reality'- that we live in a transient world- so don't feel guilty of the things which are not in your controlled.

- So if you've done your deeds to your utmost ability/ devotion then the chaos's is for the loose ends.

- Make a stringent mental statement about that & it's non-negotiable at all times.

- When you do this use the chaos's at your leverage/advantage and when the right time arrives command it & break it & establish order in your life according to your customized need.
- Easier said than done,
- I know, but if you be brave enough to do this=> next time onwards chaos will be scared of you or it will try to change it's pattern, in that case repeat the same.

Saying 'No'/ Making People Unhappy-

This is the biggest & most important art to achieve a sense of satisfaction & content in your work/life/existence.

You cannot please everyone no matter who you are and whatever you do.

This you know & easier said than done but if you want to be focussed & achieve your goals in life. It is important that you start saying ' NO' to people.

It takes time to get used to this but if you truly want to be successful you need to be severely focussed & in order to be focussed you need to set your priorities right by that I mean to be able to say 'NO' to everyone or everything except the most important prioritised task at hand that you have decided to do at that specific moment.

Most of the people will always be unhappy with whatever you do or not to do, so don't bother be ruthless & say NO

Once you start doing this in practice, you will see that how much time, money , emotions & peace you will save.

This is actually what is called as investing in yourself.

Your all thoughts should be constructive to build your own life cause if you are not happy with yourself, no one will come to save you, be ruthless in building one 'self, of course not harming others but building one's life.

Struggle(in + out)/ Regimental approach-

As Buddha said this 'world is of Suffering' So whoever takes birth will have to face struggle & obstacles but the degree of sufferings depends upon your minds strength.

Don't take suffering as only pain cause the learning you will get from it is limitless if you see through the reality of society & people & act accordingly in future too.

Your ability to take suffering & keep moving forward will determine your success in life.

If you make up your mind to enjoy suffering while thinking it's the preparation for coming good times.

The good times will taste 1000 times better after this phase- then you win life my friend.

Struggles will be inner and outer from society & other people be indifferent to these, everything is temporary except the change. So enjoy this short period of our existence in this life.

Regimental approach-

History is full of men & women who achieved the unthinkable in a period of time by building and following regimental approach on regular basis.

- Build a non-negotiable routine.
- Use stationery if it helps like-Colour pen, Highlighters, Note pads, Sticky Notes, Sticky pads, Journals, Flags, Affirmations=> This will definitely facilitate & steer your everyday productivity.

Workout & Meditate-

This is non-negotiable even if you put 10-15 minutes. It will compound the benefit over a period of time.

- Take Cold Showers-
- Make positive affirmations in the morning & before sleep.
- Believe in almighty & pray even if you are an atheist. Believe in the creation power & pray to that for abundance.
- Just like in the book ' Atomic Habit' the author shows experimental results of winners and growth that small habits/ changes on regular basis might not feel too much at the moment but over one year or a period of time, it makes the difference between a winner and

other competitor's. Accumulated small changes yields compound effect- it completely changes the person.

- Another Japanese Concept called Kaizen- incremental small changes over a period time will induce a big change & it is the process which differentiates a pro & armature, a master and a novice. So everyday plan before, what you will do, when you will do, how will you do, no matter if all the objectives doesn't go as plan but you will feel great when you experience the change.

- 'This is the real secret of mastery & learning anything'

Meditation-

- This is mostly a busyness now but it is the single most effective teaching if you practice it regularly you will achieve mental patterns, brain waves for peace, learning, concentration, focus.
- Meditation material & how to do it is freely available in the internet.
- There are a few types of meditation for example- Mindful meditation, Chakra-meditation, OM-chanting meditation, Breathing meditation(focussing on the breath) etc. etc. Choose one that suits you, start with baby steps with breath work...Focus on the inhaling and exhaling.
- Art of Living masters says ' Meditation is the subtle art of doing nothing'.
- Some sources to study mind & concentration-
- Patanjali's Yoga Sutra=> ' The Best'-If you can perceive it completely.
- Mihali Csikzentmihalyi' s book 'FLOW'- which credits Patanjali's Yogasutra & which enunciates that there is a state OF MIND called 'FLOW' IN WHICH WE ACHIEVE ULTIMATE FOCUS AND PRODUCTIVITY.

3...2..1. Focus

- If the challenges & skill is at par almost the same we achieve this state. If challenge is higher than skill, then we get rattled & if skill is higher than challenge then we get bored.

- There are ample sources from reputed Universities like Harvard and Stanford which clearly show from experimental data that meditation changes neural chemistry. Changes brain structure & makes you more happy, content & focus.

- Neuroplasticity is a concept that brain can change structure and function based on habits & certain practices, so it is your super power to change yourself.

- Also recommended if time permits to read vedanta & Upanishads.

- As said by Swami Vivekananda-The difference between an ordinary and extra-ordinary person is the degree of concentration.

Mind-mapping-

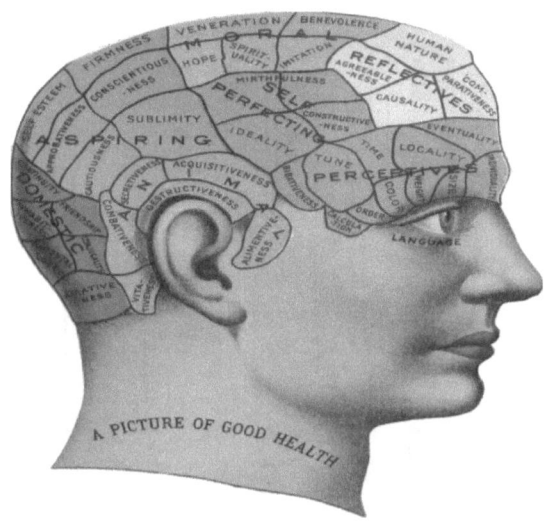

Mind mapping is the technique by which you can map large amounts of data in a flowchart or metaphoric (in every sense of use of this term) or simple key word or key visual ques in your head customised for your recall - It should be prepared from your mental scape for you only-=> slang, sex, rhyme , anything any word created for your understanding. Draw pictures, flow-charts, arrow-connection if needed. -

Your Mind Map is your mind map so make your mind map according to your convenience and optimization, use your imagination.

20   3...2..1. Focus

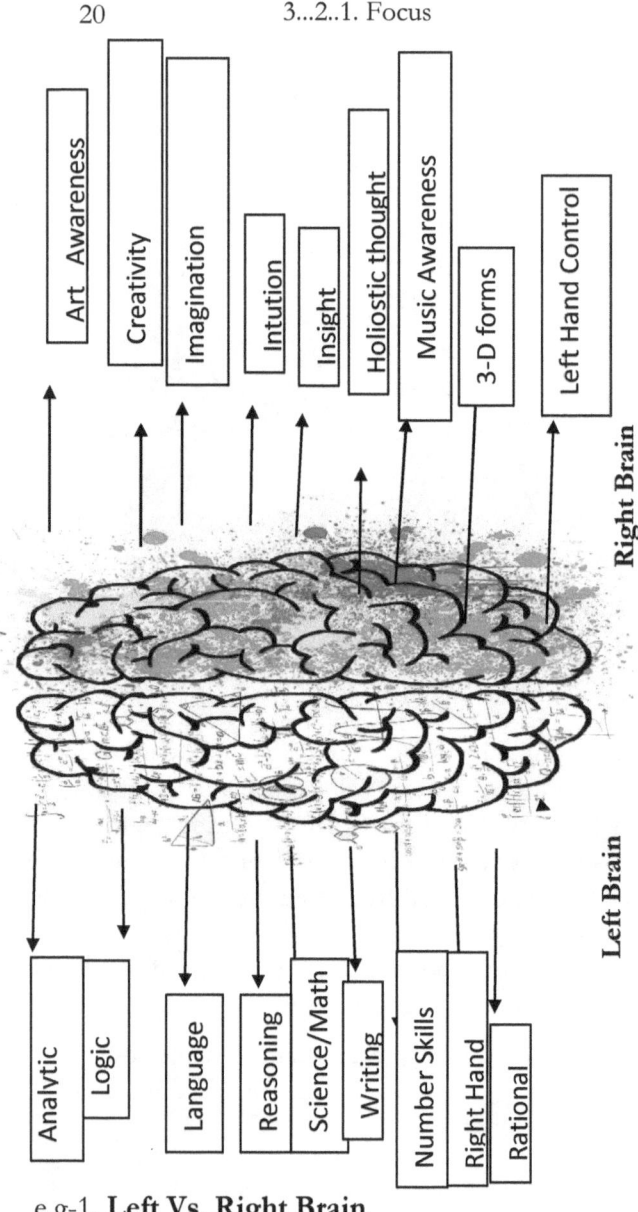

e.g-1. **Left Vs. Right Brain**

2. Divisions of Biological Sciences-

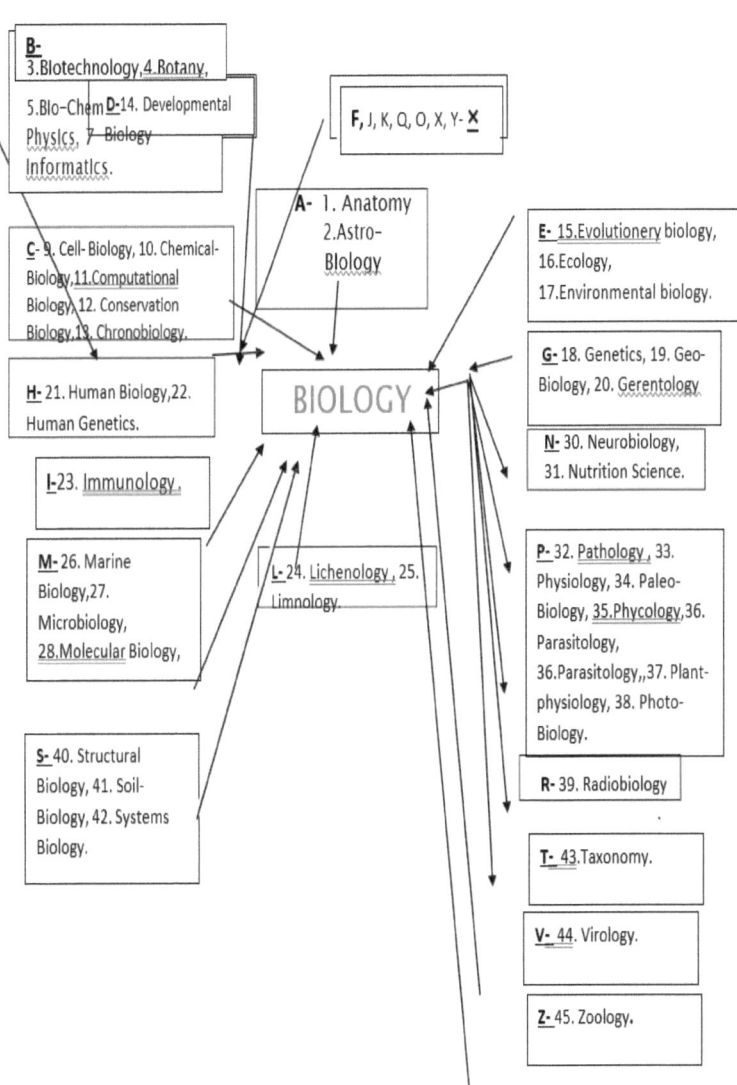

3...2..1. Focus

[Add according to your knowledge and this is a task complete the mind map by adding details regarding the informations of the above mentioned divisions.]

Mnemonics-

One of the best ways to recall & put some large bits of data/informations into your long term memory.

Again use your imagination to engulf a large numbers of important in your head by-

- Using the target data take bits and pieces of the data/information into your long term memory.

- Again use your imagination to engulf a large numbers of important informations in your head by-

- Using the target data take bits and pieces of the data and arrange in chronological r logical order according to need in super-short form to recall it wheneverneeded.

- Use to connect the datas in chronological order by using chronological stories/events of stories, it's a game changer and is availlable as permanent retention if practiced in spaced repeatation technique.(Spaced repeatation will be discussed later).

e.g- My teacher when I was in class 9 preparing for state board exams in 2005/2006.He introduced me with this magic. It's not that I have never used it unintentionally but this was an intentional introduction / application & then, then it began=>

e.g- To remember the macronutrients needed in Human Body.

Macro-nutrients-

1. Carbon(C)
2. Hydrogen(H).
3. Oxygen(O)
4. Nitrogen(N)
5. Sulfur(S)
6. Magnesium(Mg)
7. Calcium(Ca)
8. FERROUS-Iron(Fe)
9. Phosphorous(P).
10. Potassium(K).

He told me his secret, now I am sharing it-

CHONS MG CA FE P K=> Kons M ag Ca Fe P K (Pronounce it in this order separately for each underline set).

This is not an audiobook. So, follow my instructions=> Pronounce separately the separate underlines as per they re marked below=>

CHONS   Mg   Ca   Fe   P   K

(Kons) (Mag) (Ka) (F E) (P) (K)

(Separate Pronunciation)

By this method I have memorised many long and diverse data.

For example the moment he taught me that I applied it to micro-nutrients of human- body according to my creativity like-

Micronutrients-

1. Silicon (Si)
2. Molibdinum (Mo)
3. Cuprum/ Copper (Cu)
4. Bromin (B)
5. Manganese (Mn)
6. Zinc (Zn)

>>>> Si Mo Cu B Mn Zn (Simocu B Mnzn).

Sub-Concious Mind-

Suggest to read about below mentioned topics on your own-

1. Affirmations , 2. Self-Talk, 3. Prayer, 4. Binural beats, 5. Subliminal Frequency & 6.Placebo.

Read if you can- Dr. Joseph Murphy's writtings about Sub-Concious mind.

In Psychology there are mainly three types of Human Mind in terms of conciousness as parameter.

A.   Concious Mind-

The everyday information processing, Level-1 mind- can be felt it's presence when you think, Soliloquy etc., responsible for reactions and receptions of normal ques.

B.   Sub-Concious Mind-

Most important in shaping character, Behaviour response to events.

Shapes every determinants of destiny based on triggered programmed efforts/ karma to manifest destiny.

This is the place where subliminal/binural massages are targeted and received.

Busyness corporations, ad-agencys, policy makers use this technique to tap into the core of our concious choices by feeding the Sub-concious.

That is why positive affirmations, self-talk of belief and other above mentioned stuff like prayer, Mantra, programmes your mind to do great things.

This is the sole reason why propaganda and subversion plays a huge role in geo- politics to manipulate public - opinion.

Hitler's propaganda minister Goethels told ' If you state lie's again and again it is perceived as truth'- the same feeding of sub-concious. It is said that the mind conditioning in positive pursuits if done in highest efficiency you can break your limits become supirior in any given pursuit.

So don't take negative garbage- Choose your choice of elixir/poison- choice should be your according to your goals.

Unconcious collective / Collective Unconcious-

Carl Gustavo Jang famous French psychologist & these days the brilliant Dr. Jordan Peterson states-

Civilizational/ Societal/ Racial collection of thoughts/ thought patterns/ believes are transferred genetically/ geographically/ Geographically/ Culturally/ Socially etc. - which may be good for your goals or met but you should try to identify these patterns/ limits & try to have a rational/ objective analysis of the limitations & take actions by using or eliminating them conciously.

The more you succeed in doing above mentioned stuff the more you will be ahead of your time & be a leader, a vissionary a vanguard of change for good.

There is a genre of Yoga called Kundalini yoga-

Representing serpentine energy of our reproductive/ creative fluids- which when not wasted comes up thorugh spine and after rigourous practice & this is the same rigourous practice of sages through sadhana to go into samadhi- when this reaches a specific portion of the brain-stem it releases a jack-pot of hormonal/bio-chemical treassures- unleashing big-bang of bliss/euphoria far supirior than sex, this very force is the creative energy/ power by which we create or change mark our impression in the human existence.

In his brillian book Maj. Gen. G.D. Bakshi (Indian Army Vet.) advocates for this force & states this force/ energy is responsible for charisma in world famous icons/ leaders of the field to influence the mass conciousness & change the course of history.

Also it is evident to get leissure time to harness this creative force in isolation or seclusion like sages used to do in forests to master & use creative energy to become supirior in any chosen field & lead.

Morphogenetic Field Theory-

Rupert Sheldrake, a brilliant scientist advocated that our conciousness are connected.

For example he states whereever any breakthrough/event/ invention first comes out it is observed that somewhere or the other in the planet of the same species same is repeated it's like breaching thresold limits as a species as a whole. For example- Invention of radio-transmission-though Marconi got Nobel for it, it's well known reported a few more men discovered it before/after him without having any connections with him- It's named ' Morphogenetic Field Theory'--It sits well with Jang collective unconcious--- Why I am mentioning this cause if the above is true, you already have the talent/ ability to do any achievement/task that already has been achieved or done, just try your best- never consider your mind to be inferior to anyone you are supirior inside out.

Work-Out-

Umpteen number of material is availlable on the net & on the books regarding this but I will share my 2 cents-

1. Start with whatever you have with what you can do-- whenever, wherever- that doesn't kill you makes you stronger.

2. Above was the worst case scenario action, now--

3. Follow a routine-- do workouts as 15 minutes if you truly don't have- make time.

- Push-Ups-20/25 sets each-2/4 sets.

- Sit-Ups- 10/20 sets each-2 sets at least.

- Chin-up/ Pull up- As per strength/ customised - but do perfectly even if you do one.

- Arch/ Chakrasan-(Do standing stance -if you can) for spinal flexibility & spinal flexibility & many more fast benefits.

- Can use little 20 pound dumbbells for bicep training/curls.

- Do Hindu push-ups if you can - for man specially.

- Use variations like-using push-up bars/one-hand push-up/use any place to heightened push-ups/use parks natural workout infrastructure to increase difficulty.

- Use stairs.

- Run in morning/evening as per convenience.

- Above mentioned techniques should be ascended as per progress/age/sex & abilities.

- If you can manage to do the above simple exercises along with healthy diet and rest-- you will too have a healthy/strong body in 3 months guaranteed.

DOSE-[THE REWARD CIRCUIT]-

- We are all bio-chemical machines everything has a beginning from a chemical secretion in the body.

- DOSE-

D- Dopamine- Pleasure Hormone.

O-Oxytocin- Bonding Hormone.

S-Serotonin-

E- Endorphins- Feel Good Hormones.

Hormones are chemicals massagers which regulate, Initiate, influence or end every biological actions which produce, maintain, deplete the system through cascade of events which we call human body or more precisely a human body.

Evolutionary or creation whatever the initiator of this systems is may be not completely understood yet but we know the pattern of it's working through modern neuroscience at least presumably for most of the part.

Any hard work or sacrifices, suffering demands any kind of reward set in the mind of the concerned.

we are all hardwired to respond most vividly in terms of pain or pleasure marker.

Dopamine-

- Food /sex/ winning/ alcohol/ certain drugs/ happiness/ anything big/ molecule of more/ achievement etc.- all are connected with the pleasure hormone dopamine.

- Present in the form of L-DOPA- precursor of the Dopamine neurotransmitter- previously thought of as only precursor of nor- epinephrine & epinephrine but also an important probably one of the most important neurotransmitter released from substantia nigra, ventral tegmental area, hypothalamus of the brain.

- Dopamine will want more & more the progress & expansion of human race in this physical realm can be directly attributed to this molecule of magnificence.

- It is the sole reason why humans are conquerors & the highest form of existence in the planet earth.

- The more you like something or something which is responsible for your existence or passing of your genes is rewarded by this molecule. (i.e. Sex).

- But modern day has hacked this system by digital means- fooling your reward circuit through social media, internet & mother of all distractions- Sex.

- That's why the circuitry which is given or developed to achieve greatness is being compromised by fake representations of audio-visual stimuli.

- Modern men are getting weaker cause the main circuitry which is responsible for efforts & taking sufferings on purpose to achieve goals have been compromised to a large extent.

- That's why they are becoming frequent 'Fappers' & not 'Achievers'.

- Porn has taken over world as the biggest busyness after arms & ammunitions.

- Energy of building and conquering empires/creations are now in a fantasy world being wasted.

- Porn and repression of modern men in terms of fake equality is the reason of increase in crime in the world.

- But the good news is you can always take charge of your life and hack this reward circuitry to your advantage.

- The more you win the more dopamine surge occurs to reward you more, the more motivated you become. The more you loose the less you get of pleasure hormone- the less you are likely to try again.

- This hormone is responsible for the sole motivation as we call it.
- This is the connection between- winning streak of a champion who gets more motivated & fierce in any field after every successful endeavours & vice versa is also true.
- It's a two-edged sword.
- Addiction/obsession/efforts/achievements all inception from the same molecular mechanism.
- Here's the deal the more you get surge by a task/drug/sex-addiction quantity- next time you will have to outperform your achievements/
- drugs/ sex/ addiction to achieve the same level of pleasure hormone otherwise it will not feel the same/ waste- because dopamine seeks all or nothing slots at least most of the time.
- This is why achiever amplifies his/ her achievements & addiction makes addictor more addicted to lose his self-Nothing matters except that feeling of satisfaction of reaching the feeling/ happiness/bliss at the pinnacle--
- Brain equates old happy habits with survival.

Oxytocin-

- 'The love hormone '/ 'The Bonding hormone'- essential in child birth.

- Breast feeding after birth releases oxytocin which in turn initiates bonding- a very special one- mother-child bond/ parent-child one.

- This hormone creates bonding-- promotes trust/ empathy in a relationship.

- It releases with physical affection like- kissing, cuddling, sex etc.

- Oxytocin is produced in the hypothallamus & is secreted into the blood stream by the posterior pituitary gland.

Serotonin-

This hormone & neuro-transmitter helps in regulation of mood as well as sleep, appetite, digestion, learning ability and memory formations..

Released in sunlight/ nauseated condition triggers it.

In the CNS (Central Nervous System) nervous system- it is almost exclusively produced in neurons originating in the raphe nuclei located in the midline of the brain- stem, these serotonin producing neurons form the largest and most complex efferent system in the human brain.

Endorphins-

Body's natural pain reliever/ pain killer. - Released during workout/ sunlight/ reward seeking activities.

- Mood enhancer makes you feel high

- Endorphins are released from the pituitary gland typically in response to pain and can act in both the Central Nervous System and the peripheral nervous system.

- With proper diet, exercise, getting out running in sunlight, meditation staying away from addiction-

- This complex of multivariant productive outcome will

naturally perform and grow when your goal oriented and naturally do 'SMART' work.

Specific Measurable Achievable Realistic Time bound

How to use/ hack DOSE system

1.Meditation, 2. Work-out-exercise, 3. Green Vegetables, 4. Protein in diet, 5. Cardio exercise, 6. Bonding with wife/ partner, 7. Proper rest, 8. Avoiding energy sucking people as far as possible, 9. Daily Microscope, 10. Dark chocolate/ sweets.

- These will ultimately trigger this reward complex adequately/ optimally to become an achiever, doer, problem solver, happy motivated high energy focused individual who gets things done. (August 2021)

Habit Formation/ Getting shit done-

It is found from evidence based research that any new habit takes 21 days of repetition to make the task/ritual/ work a habit & to break a one/ replace one it takes almost 45 days.

In my opinion it is highly personalised life-stage/ situation oriented system management issue can't be generalised.

So accordingly with iron-mind set start constructive efforts your daily habits. You will feel in your mind & heart that it's done and something.

You will feel in your mind & heart that it's done & something is part of your daily schedule-- Here what matters is consistent honest efforts. Not every day will be same but make sure you achieve your daily tasks. Keep daily goals achievable according to your ability. If you in any day you couldn't achieve daily goals don't panic, make sure you have a buffer or overcome it the next day or in coming days. This sense of satisfaction that you are in the process of progress will increase dopamine release & you will be motivated even more.

Though I would suggest do not depend upon motivation cause you will not have it all day all the time. It's like a muscle use it or loose it.

Suggest to complete micro tasks with honesty even if you do not feel like doing it. --- That is an hallmark of an warrior/ achiever.

- Getting shit done is one of the most important parts of becoming extra-ordinary/ super productive.

- When you don't feel like getting up in the morning or doing something.

- You should mandatorily do it to feel what my body or mind did'nt wanted to do- this will make you understand that your consciousness is beyond body and mind- this is the mindset of a true champion- Nothing, Nothing, Nothing can stop you after assimilating this truth.

- I would like to share a story regarding this, owing to my work I have talked with lot of Army, Navy and Airforce veterans-one story by an ex-Air force men told me that there is a ritual or unwritten rule- that whenever a plane gets crashed or aborted due to unforseen events they make sure after that they do it even more and more the same task with the same equipment's or conditions- it destroys fear and amplifies the confidence.

- So, whatever the things that are impeding/ blocking your performance to the fullest potential make sure it's done/solved/ destroyed if necessary & get your shit done always...always.

Pleasing only thyself / Stop being a people pleaser-

Please only thyself/ yourself & feed your ego in a positive way build it for growth & set your standards build a legacy.

You cannot please everyone. The people who wants to please everyone. The people who wants to please everyone almost always end-up pleasing no-one & losing self-worth/ respect & peace of mind.

So, do not harm anyone just do your every goal/ task honestly for you and your families future not to please or satisfy anyone else.

Only when you truly are happy & successful then only you can make changes to others life, if you want to... to make others happy.

- Your first priority should be always you.

- It's not selfish, it's a duty of you to first consolidate and prosper yourself then the bigger goals, if anyone can come into front.

- The more virtuous and successful you will be, the more likely you will have a positive impact in the world/ society. First build yourself & if destiny has it you will make bigger changes/ impact.

- Become an inspiration among the people of your starata in the society.
- Your competition is with you.

Diversify-

After sometime while following a regimental routine- change/diversify the tasks.

Not just study- balance life. Everything is connected & works best if it's in best possible permutation-combination balanced form.

Do everything in moderation except efforts to achieve your goals.

Diversify work, study, workout. Mix things- try to achieve an holistic improvement in the long run.

- Learn music or self-run any instrument/ language/ travel.

- Try to achieve new learning.

- Linguistics & music instrument learning develops new brain connections for better learning memory.

- There are umpteen amounts of studies suggesting, those who learn new music instrument or language or active in problem solving has better neural network & brain health-- severely lesser risks of Alzheimer & other cognitive disorder/ degenerations.

Diversifying daily tasks with different tasks & processes will increase reward systems activity & will cut monotonous feeling which the brain hates.

Understanding Brains Formation-

Brain is the most astonishing and enigmatic structure that living organisms harbour.

Memory is one of the most important faculties that humans have. Here we will enunciate the structure & function of brain responsible for memory formation & retention to get to comprehend what actually goes on inside the skull.

Memory-

There are normally two types of memories-
I. Short-term memory &
II. Long-term memory.

Usually when we talk about memory or remembering things, we are referring to explicit memory which is consciously recalled.

Explicit memories can be episodic, meaning they relate to experiences or 'episodes' in your life (a particular holiday or the first time you were biten by dog) or they are semantic, relating to facts or data (e.g.- the brain has about 90 billion neurons).

Long-term memory-

Long-term memories are mainly of two types- Explicit (Conscious) & Implicit (unconscious).

Unconscious memories can be procedural- learned motor skills- practice based. e.g.- How to ride a cycle, learning piano.

Implicit memories result from priming, which occurs when exposure to one influences your brains response to another.

e.g.- Associated words, pattern, recognition etc.

Explicit- Stored in-

Hippocampus	Neo-Cortex	Amygdyla
Located in the brains temporal lobe(episodic memories etc.	Largest part of the cerebral cortex- outside surface of the brain. Distinctive in higher mammals for its uniquely appearance- in humans- higher spatial recognition, sensory perception. Languages.	An almond shaped structure in the brains temporal lobe/ attaches emotional significance to memory.

Implicit- Stored in-

Basal Ganglia	Cerebellum
The Basal Ganglia are structures lying deep within the brain and are involved in a wide range of	A separate structure located at the rear base of the brain, most important in fine motor control.
processes such as emotions, movements, learning etc.	

Working Memory-

Prefrontal Cortex-

The prefrontal cortex is the part of the neo-cortex that sits at the very front of the brain. It is the most recent addition to the mammalian brain, involved in many advanced cognitive functions.

Left- Prefrontal Cortex- work in verbal memory.
Right –Prefrontal Cortex-Spatial working memory.

Short term to Long term memory consolidation-

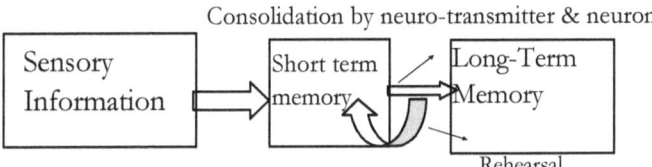

- ➢ Sensory inputs- Cortical neurons- Hippocampus to strengthening cortical -synaptic connection- Practice/ Repetition- Hippocampus- Back to cortex for permanent storage.

- ➢ From Pre-frontal cortex to hippocampus the Short-Term Memory comes from neural network & then rehearsal & spaced repetition after consolidation- Long term memory. It's transferred to Prefrontal Cortex for permanent storage.

How to improve Memory-

1. Meditate.
2. Exercise- Aerobic exercise-s Stopping Hippocampus shrinking. ⟶ Brain Plasticity/ Neuro plasticity.
3. Write (writing is thinking)
4. High quality relationships.
5. Read…Read…Read.
6. Adopt the growth mind set (motivate yourself, stay fit & positive).
7. Challenge your mind.- with the right amount of challenge according to your present skill level.
8. Have right amount of stress/ anxiety is good but not panicking beyond the healthy limit.
9. Sleep-well.

How we know- Patient H.M case-

Brain Research- How do we know what we know about brain structures and their functions in maintaining and forming memory.

Most researched and Studied brain in the history of mankind.

On September 1, 1953, time stopped for Henry Molaison. For roughly 10 years, the 27-year-old had suffered severe seizures. By 1953, they were so debilitating he could no longer hold down his job as a motor winder on an assembly line. On September 1, Molaison allowed surgeons to remove a thumb-sized section of tissue from each side of his brain. It was an experimental procedure that he and his surgeons hoped would quell the seizures wracking his brain.

As a young boy cracked skull>>>Seizures>>> Dropped out of school>>Dr. Scaville>> Dare Devil Surgeon>>Did Partial Lobotomy>>Initially seizures stopped>> But after few times>> Short-term memory loss>> Started repeating behaviour/ tasks/ food eating>> forgetting everything>> 15 minutes recall period.

- New clue of distinction>> Short term Vs. Long term memory>> Different storage plans>> without hippocampus>> No long term storage>> It was later on found that Basal Ganglia and Cerebellum were intact and as a result>> Procedural memory was intact>> But declarative memory>> Dates/Number lost.

- Most studied brain after demise 2000 slides were made.

Emergency studying-

In this case I can give you real solutions cause whatever major exams, I have given & passed or exceled are almost 90 % of them were under some uncontrolled emergency eventuality. But there is silver lining- you will not be able to out-perform all the emergencies all the times if you don't take isolation.

➤ Always try to avoid this emergency but if it's unavoidable- then follow the below instructions.

Must do to tame emergency and perform

I. **Calm your mind**- Always remember you are not in control of the surroundings/events- be at peace with yourself. Become like a cold blooded hunter waiting for perfect time to attack, ever present and focussed.

II. **Control which can be controlled-** Don't try to control uncontrollable things.

III. Always have a back-up plan if the goal is of a long term.

IV. Improvise according to the unfolding situations- always try to stick to your objectives.

V. Consolidate all the materials which are truly important or non-negotiable & complete them according to the improvised design- there is no such thing as a perfectly perfect planning or technique- you finish your objectives based on circumstances- in a calm mind- be fearless.

VI. Do not think of a perfect approach because there are none.

VII. Be fearless- outcome is not in your hand you just give your best according to the situation.

VIII. Lesser the time –you bring most important things in one place—focus on priority only at least in first instance.

IX. Take deep breaths & believe in your previous preparations.

X. Have faith and play your part to the best of your capabilities.

XI. Don't repent wasted time, it's not wasted- it's your fuel for success.

"Rest assured you'll do well for sure".

Fear of failure/ Unwanted eventualities-

"If you truly fear failures & act to stop it, you will almost never fail- it's that strong."

Break the vicious cycle of mind by not taking it seriously when it doubts your hard work & starts a recap of your not so anticipated unwanted outcomes It's a façade- defence mechanism designed to protect you instead it sabotages growth. You cannot control what you cannot control.

" Whatever happens, happens"-

Once done don't waste time change the future by planned organised actions. Make fear your fuel & by defeat it by proving it wrong.

Control which can be controlled- rest is not in your hand- your actions are only in your hand.

Honest to thyself-

No one's special, not even you—everyone including you need to work-hard to be good at something.

But the same logic can be reversed & stated as everyone is special, you are special in a unique way your genetic, psychological scope is unique. So a special creation i.e. you in this spectacular combination yielding you as an living entity will not be created again… Like they say…

"what we do in life echoes into eternity"

- ➢ So be honest to accept your level, aptitude, situation, I.Q etc & build from there one step at a time.

- ➢ Work to improve the weak skills.

- ➢ A good student may be genetically or infrastructurally gifted and had already made the journey- you are supposed to start.

-may be say he / she's in 80 % to achieving expertise after 3 years- studying on an average 3 hours/ day.

If you want to beat him/her with in short period- try 5/6/8 hours' average for 1 year take the pain of discipline- you will topple the topper- most of the chances are you will achieve expertise before them.

So don't compare yourself with other- you start your journey as per your unique style with defined goals. - be honest to yourself at all the times.

Focus Techniques-

- ✓ If it's necessary, have some rituals before starting study.
- ✓ Chant 'mantra' as it focuses the mind.
- ✓ Meditate before study.
- ✓ Take deep breath & start.
- ✓ Do not take repeated breaks in short-time- I am against the popular notion/belief of taking break- after 20 minutes- it is distracting if you truly want achieve something.
- ✓ Can use pomodoro technique that – one-hour complete non-distracted study then a little break then again back to grinding.
- ✓ Try to find isolation, if you can, leisure is the mother of creativity.
- ✓ Try to have deep focus of at least 4-5 hours daily, if you want to ace any competitive exam/sports/any task.
- ✓ Be absolutely ' No Mind'- think and act only for task at hand in given time.

Psychadelics/Nootropics/Mind Renewal-

This portion is only for academic & understanding purposes not to be considered without medical/ expert prescription.

Psychedelics-

Any substance/drug/ vegetable/ fruit/ edible/ non-edibles which alters or have the capability of altering/ expanding neuro-chemistry/ consciousness/ perception can be broadly termed as psychadelics. e.g-

D.m.t (Dimethyl tryptamine)- The spirit molecule, psilocybin mushroom, meo toad venom, marijuana, acacia sp., Amenita muscaria etc..

New findings-

I want my readers to have an open mind & get an overall perspective of a matter in every angle of quantifiable observations.

D.MT.- Is presumed to be the mother of all & presumed to be secreted when we die from pineal gland to act as a gateway to other dimensions, it has been studied extensively by Dr. Straussman and still it's being studied in several top universities. It is stated as a chemical gateway, though it's produced from liver too but can't reach brain because of an inhibitor enzyme which prohibits it to breach blood-brain barrier. All sorts of fantastic unbelievable experiences can be heard from people taking d.mt artificially.

Ayahuasca-

An ancient Amazonian tree bark ritual where in the bark is used to create a drink which creates hallucinogenic experiences and it's active ingredient is also d.mt.

- Everyone experiencing the ritual or d.mt have experienced either bliss, hallucination, ego-death, trauma-healing, anxiety-depression healing, pain healing or fearful encounters with unexplainable entities, organisms etc.

- But, it rewires the brain, kills ego and trauma, re designes serotinergic system ,, kills depression and pain etc. which modern medicine does not seem to heal for long time.

- All the information's are available in the public domain & in no way advise to try this are just information's of how brain can be rewired what are the holistic information's are available worldwide and how brain can be rewired in shorter periods of time.

- It's just fascinating but for some reasons d.m.t and all these stuff is banned in most of the countries & India too. Modern psychologists are looking/ experimenting into this substance for trauma-healing.

Nootropics-

Nootropics are the drugs that can be termed as the cognitive enhancers-both natural and artificial.

If you have seen the 2011, Bradley Cooper film " Limitless"- you will have a good understanding of the nootropics.

Tapping into the reward/ learning circuit it promotes less distraction, alertness, focus, learning for a specified time period.

For example- again this is only for knowledge and understanding not prescribed, can be done after expert advice.

Ayurvedic	**Allopathic**
Brahmi extract/ liquid, *Ginkgo biloba* extract/ liquid, Ashwagandha extract/ liquid..etc.	Only can be prescribed by a registered practitioner- 1. Modafinil*. 2. Provigil. Etc.

- Brilliant drug- Can't be taken without expert prescription- Super alertness without side-effect. Taken by High performers/ fighter pilots/ med students etc. If you are suffering from A.D.H.D- Attention Deficit Hyperactivity Disorder.

Diagnosed for the above then may be Doctor will prescribe it.

In no way I advocate any one to use this but it's for holistic knowledge, so that any normal person can have knowledge to take better decisions. In this era of Distractions and competition it's needed to think differently.

" Normal healthy brain is always best to have without any drug/ supplement."

Your Brain is the most sophisticated chemical factory whatever drugs/ substance works in your brain is just merely facilitating the processes that your brain is naturally capable of achieving. They just bind to the specific receptors which are already there meaning if you did'nt had those rceeptors on the first hand for something already there it should have been absent. I think you get my point. Do the breath work and research by yourself in the path of self-discovery. It's your journey you will have to take the journey by yourself.

Focus on the system development, the outcome wIll follow-

➢ **GIta-** Best working manual for focus in front of

massacre like distracting situations. Hindu scripture 'Gita' was delivered in the battle-field, which states- focus only on the efforts (karma) not on the outcome. You cannot control the outcome.

- "Karm karo fal ki chinta mat karo"- Do your work, don't think/ worry of the result).

- MIracles happen, If you don't have any expectatIons- karma Is your reward.

- EverythIng Is extra by product.

- Enjoy the moments, Enjoy even boardom.

- **CollectIve UncooncIous- Carl Gustavo Jang – facIng bullIes and destroyIng It-**

This concept is mentioned here in order to better equip the reader against unconscious impediments which they harbour without their conscious knowledge-

Carl Gustavo Jang in his analytical psychology mentioned this fascinating concept wherein he mentioned that-

"The collective unconscious is a universal version of the personal unconscious, holding mental patterns, or memory traces which are shared with other members of human species (Jung, 1928)" These are expressed as per Jung as archetypes-

He mentioned 4 archetypes-

- The Persona (or mask)- out ward projection.

- The Anima or Animus- mirror image of biological sexes.

- Shadow- Animal Side of personality both creative and destructive power.

- The Self- A sense of self/ Unity in expression.

The cultural/ colonial/ trans-generational trauma or any attribute is imprinted in that specific community/ geography etc., in their collective unconscious & without the person's knowledge- shapes his psyche & believe system.

Solution

Not any proven solution exists but one of the first step is to know & acknowledge the issue & try to get above the detected limitations of unconscious consciously, after several attempts the imprint changes or modifies for better.

Those who are able to do this they are the unbiased thinkers, the vanguards of progress.

"Don't let past trauma whether conscious or unconscious impede your growth— Acknowledge and defeat it".

Positive Affirmations-

Whenever in doubt or not feeling the fire- try affirmations- sharp, clean, mental, specific, big positive affirmations- feed sub-concious with positive thoughts & affirmations-

e.g-

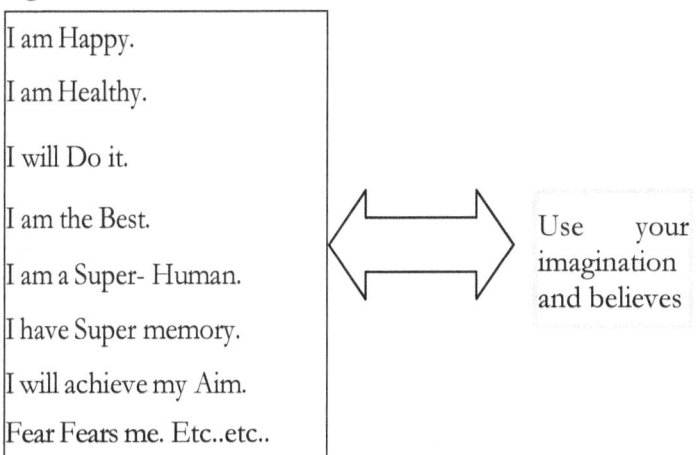

I am Happy.

I am Healthy.

I will Do it.

I am the Best.

I am a Super- Human.

I have Super memory.

I will achieve my Aim.

Fear Fears me. Etc..etc..

Use your imagination and believes

It works like magic specially in the morning after getting up and before going to sleep at night.

Few Techniques Of Study In Snippets-

1. Pomodoro technique,
2. Deep Focus
3. Anki-method
4. Spaced-repeatation
5. Sticky Note
6. Writing after reading
7. Active recall
8. Study in candle light/ study lamp in the darkness.

Flow-

'Flow' Is a state of effIcIently doIng a task & It fIrst came or advocated by Japanese scIentIst msIhaI psIktsenmIhaI In hIs book 'flow' that flow Is the optimal or effortless productIve stage of actIons when equal levels of challenge meets equal skIll levels set. Any devIatIon/elevatIon from that equIlIIbrIum wIll destroy flow state.

Too much challenge than skIlls & vIce versa = no 'flow' state.

Patanjali's yogasutra-

This is the best manual for concentration & focus- msihai also mentioned this in his 'flow' book.

How to focus mind is meticulously elaborated in this scripture.

A founder of Ashtanga Yoga tradition sage Patanjali in 500 B.C wrote a text containing 196 sutras in Sanskrit which is known as 'Yogasutras'.

- One sutra forms one statement. Statements are in Sanskrit.

- Sutras harbour multivariant meaning in compacted form.

- To explain or perceive these sutras it takes expertise in both Sanskrit and in philosophy of yoga to get a perspective which can be justified with the authors intent.

Parts-

I. Samadhi Pada- 51 Sutras-

First chapter of Samadhi Pada starts with first sutra-' Atha Yoga Anushasanam— Atha means now (I-1).

Anushasanam means discipline. " Now is the discipline of yoga".

- **Second sutra enunciates definition of yoga.- " Yogaha Chitta Vritti Nirodhah (I- 2)—**

Chitta means mind, Vritti means modifications of mind., Nirodhah means control.

Yoga is to control the modifications (states of emotion/experience/ perception) of mind.

- **Third sutra is about ultimate achievement of yoga--- Tada Drashtuh Swarupe Awasthanam (I-3).**

Tada means—after that.

Drashtuh means—the seen.

Swarupe means--- State of self or soul.

Awasthanam means--- Resides.

After that (Control of functioning of mind) the seen establishes himself into true state of being.

In first chapter Patanjali explains five types of vritties (types of modifications of mind)—

Also Patanjali talks about seven paths to achieve the ultimate objective of controlling the uncontrollable mind.

One of the most effective of these is the Omkar chanting.

In First chapter Patanjali also explains the various types of Samadhi (Ultimate state of achievement in yoga).

Sabija Samadhi & Nirbija Samadhi.

Sabija is further subdivided into 'Sampradyat & 'Asampradayat'.

Sampradayat is further subdivided into four types— Savitarka, Savichara, Sananda, Sasmita.

Nirbija Samadhi is the ultimate state of achievement in yoga.

II. **Sadhana Pada-** 55 sutras-

In the second chapter, Patanjali explains the tools & techniques to achieve the ultimate goal of yoga.

All EIGHT PARTS OF Ashtanga yoga are explained by Patanjali in this chapter.

Yama- Social discipline,

Niyama- Self-discipline,

Asana- Yoga postures.

Pranayama- Breath control.,

Pratyahara- Sense withdrawal., Dhaarana- Concentration.

Dhyana- Meditation & Samadhi- Self-realizaation are 8 (eight) steps of yoga, but in this chapter the focus is on first five steps.

III. Vibhuti Pada—56 sutars.

Remainining 3 steps of Dharana- Concentration, Dhayana-meditation & Samadhi-Self-realization are discussed in details by patanjali. All three together is called SAMYAM. Samyam on different objects leads to different achievements which are called Siddhis(perfections).

IV. Kaivalya Pada- 34 sutras.
Janmaushadhimantratapha Samdhija Sidhyaya (IV-1)---

V.

Ways to achieve ultimate states of Samadhi—

1. By Birth.
2. Mantra chanting.
3. Practicing Tapa (Austerity).
4. Practice of Yoga.

Nutrition for Memory

Nutrition is of monumental importance in Human Bodies well-being specially maintaining an healthy memory. a concise sample nutritional food habit is discussed in this chapter ...

Three main pillers of nutrition-

1. Food, 2. Medicine, 3. Supplements.

Diet (β- amyloid plaque in the brain)-

Diets high in cholesterol & fat might speed up the formation of β- amyloid plaques in the brain. These sticky protein clusters are responsible for most of the damage that occurs in the brains of people with Alzheimer's.

Food for Memory-

If saturated and trans fat are the food villains, then mono and polysaturated fats may be the hero's in the dietary war of preserving memory. In particular, the mediterranian diet, with it's menu of foods that are high in healthy unsaturated fats (olive oil, fish & nuts) has been linked to lower rates of both dementia from

Alzheimers disease & mild cognitive impairment(MCI)- the stage of cognitive decline with memory loss that frequently precedes dementia.

The Mediterranean diet includes several components that might promote Brain health.

➤ Fruits, vegetables, whole grains, fish & olive oil help improve the health of blood vessels, reducing the risk for a memory damaging stroke.

➤ Fish are high in omega-3 fatty acids, which have been linked to lower levels of β- amyloid proteins in the blood and better vascular health.

➤ Moderate Alcohol consumption raises levels of healthy high density lipo- proteins(HDL) cholesterol. Alcohol also lowers our cells resistance to insulin, allowing it to lower blood sugar more effectively. Insulin resistance has been linked to dementia.

Sample mediteranean diet-

Breakfast-

Whole grain muesli with fresh berries and almonds or 6 oz. Greek yogurt topped with blue berries.

Lunch-

Greek salad with grilled chicken or whole-grain pita with 2 tbsp. hummus & tomatoes.

Dinner—

Roasted Salmon with tomato-olive tapenade, sauted spinach with pine nuts & raisins, poached pear or boiled chicken with garlic & lemon, asparagus.

Indian Diet For Memory-

Eat food which is rich in essential fatty acids (EFA' s), Vitamin-B-complex, Vitamin-C & amino acids.

Whole grain foods (like oats, dalia, ragi) instead of refined versions like white breads). Avoid sweets and sugary foods and processed foods.

Oily fish—rich source of omega-3.

Fresh coconut- add to diet.

Milky drink for tryptophan before bed.

➢ Balance diet- fruits and vegetables.

➢ 6-8 glass of water everyday.

➢ Green vegetables.

➢ Vit-C AND B-

- Black currents, Citrus fruits, fish, green leafy, vegetables, mushrooms, peanuts, sesame seeds, eggs to rev up brain power.
- Nuts and Seeds-
- Pumpkin seeds- ZINC- Sharpening memory.
- Brain shaped walnuts- Omega-3 and essentials. Sunflower seeds.
- Berries- Helps combat short-term memory-loss. Strawberries helps in age related memory decline.

Vit-E, K and B9- folate , iron—Green vegetable--- Brain cell development, mental alertness.

Avocados, Tomatos etc.—cognitive enhancement.

Anki-method-

It's fast learning method based on flash card system. Specially used by pre-med and med students for recall.

Method- In this method you consolidate or simplify active ingredients/ words of a topic into flash-cards. So, that when after sometimes you see it, you can recall the entire topic, the way you want to recall.

- Either you can do it manually or can use Anki apps.

- This is based upon the principal of spaced repetition & active recall.

Spaced Repetition-

- Memory/ Learning/ Habit is formed in neurological cells by sheathing myelin (fat) in the neurons after trying/ efforts/ actions-- So, the more we do something once / learn something/ experience something a new myelin sheath is generated around neurons axons—If we practice something after certain spaced intervals the sheath becomes stronger & it becomes more and more permanently ingrained in that entity as traits/ habits/ skills.

- Key is to do the task in intervals after a space/ time gap this is the holy-grail of learning.

Active Recall-

- Principal of active learning.
- Actively stimulate the memory during learning process.
- Passive recall- reading, watching only.
- Feynman Technique   3R's- Read, Recite, Review.
- Psychological testing effect and is very efficient in consolidating long term memory.
- Research revealed that it is the quickest, most efficient and effective way to study written materials, at least for factual and problem solving tests.
- Said to be better than the neo-cortex which has an active recall that can use episodic information to build new semantic memories, which could mean the hippocampus plays a role in the way memories are consolidated in the neo-cortex.

Method-

- Survey-Survey or skim through the material to get an idea of what it is about.
- Question- Create some questions that you have and that you think the text might answer.
- Read- Then actively read the text, trying to answer the questions you created.
- Retreive- This is the active recall from memory the info. You learn oraly or writing.
- REVIEW- once you finish that, repeat— Summarise material.
- Some suggestions for evidence based spaced repeatation-

Time to test (remaining)	FIRST Study GAP
1 MONTH	1 WEEK
3 MONTHS	2 WEEKS
6 MONTHS	3 WEEKS
1 YEAR	1 MONTHS

10000 Hour Rule-

In the famous book 'Outliers' Malcolm Gladwell talks about 10000-hour rule of practice. In this method he states that in order to achieve mastery at anything one need to practice for 10000 hours to get better than ordinary or average and achieve expertise.

As Gladwell tells it, the rule goes like this: It takes 10000 hours of intensive practice to achieve mastery of complex skills & materials like playing the violin or getting as good as Bill Gates at programming.

Gladwell describes one central study in particular, about which he writes:

"Their research suggests that once a musician has enough ability to get into a top music school, thing that distinguishes one performer from another is how he or she works that's it."

But that's not it, according to the researchers. It's a bit more complicated when you dig into it.

Gladwell's 10000-hour rule is a bit of faulty & it's proven. It doesn't take into account same variables.

How good a student's teacher is.

Deliberate practice with feedback system & acting upon the feedback.

Time frame is customised for every individual harbouring their preconceived skills.

Erickson's research suggests that someone could practice for thousands of hours & still not be a master performer. They could be outplayed by someone who practiced less but had a teacher who showed them just what to focus on at a key moment in their practice regime.

In a 1993 paper, Ericksson & two colleges described their research into the role of "deliberate practice" in the success of violin students. As Gladwell noted, they found that it took a remarkable amount of good time on such practice--- Some 10 years' worth 10000 hours to gain mastery, but what Gladwell left out is the role of the "Deliberate" practice, meaning work under the guidance of a teacher.

Assessment and Feedback are of prime importance.

Pomodoro technique-

Is a time management method developed by Francesco cirillo in the late 1980's. Timer is used to break intervals of 25 minutes(focussing on single mindedly to a single task), then 5 minute break to refocus >>can be customised as per convenience of the concerned.

Deep-Focus-

- Is a term coined by Cal Newport in his same nomenclatured book >> 5-6 hours of deep focus in the most important knowledge or skills/ development single mindedly without any electronic/ internet/ social media to achieve big goals in short time.

- Lesser important works/ shallow works as he call it should be done in a bunch or in minimal time.

- Training brain to focus in the data-age distractions.. In my words..' Make Brains Great Again'.

Peroration

In this book enunciation of an overall perspective, eventualities, situations, processes, solutions have been discussed and in many cases you will find it's consolidation and interlinking of different subjects of study. Use these information's and insights according to your need. After analysing through this book make up your customised system for optimal focus, concentration and development. This rigorous hard/smart work to put all this concept / techniques in consolidated interlinked format to best serve the reader will be rewarded if it serves its purpose i.e. helps people achieving their goals, over-coming trauma, becoming successful & most importantly live a focused fulfilling life.

About the Author

Bhaskar Sengupta

Bhaskar has done his Masters from Science College, University of Calcutta.

Bhaskar has prepared for competetive exams for almost 5 years and cracked many Govt. exams, currently his posted in Kolkata as Assistant Audit Officer, Indian Audit and Accounts Department.

Bhaskar is an adventure enthusiast. Love the Mountains and Mixed Martial Arts. Trained in Kick Boxing. Loves to study all that is scientific and spiritual.

www.ingramcontent.com/pod-product-compliance
Lightning Source LLC
LaVergne TN
LVHW041624070526
838199LV00052B/3230